SEAHORSES

Ruby Tuesday Books

Ruth Owen

Little Acorns

Published in 2026 by Ruby Tuesday Books Ltd.

Copyright © 2026 Ruby Tuesday Books Ltd.

All rights reserved. No part of this publication may be reproduced in whole or in part, stored in any retrieval system, or transmitted in any form or by any means, electronic, mechanical, photocopying, recording, or otherwise, without written permission from the publisher.

Editor: Mark J. Sachner
Design & Production: Tammy West

Photo Credits:
Nature Picture Library: 5 (Norbert Wu), 8 (David Fleetham), 11 (Jeff Rotman), 18 (Doug Perrine), 19 (Shane Gross); Science Photo Library: 17 (Steve Gschmeissner); Shutterstock: Cover (Soonios Pro), 1 (Lemaris), 2–3, 4 (Studio 37), 6 (Roser Gari Perez), 7 (Tabooma), 9 (bluehand), 22T (Allexxandar), 22B (Bernard S Tjandra), 23B (Nina Milton); Tony Wu (Nature Picture Library): 10, 13, 15, 16, 21, 23T.

Library of Congress Control Number: 2025937138

Print (Hardback) ISBN 978-1-78856-603-2
Print (Paperback) ISBN 978-1-78856-604-9
ePub ISBN 978-1-78856-605-6

Published in Minneapolis, MN
Printed in the United States

www.rubytuesdaybooks.com

CONTENTS

Let's Dance! 4

Glossary 22

Index 24

Let's Dance!

Female seahorse

Male seahorse

Under the ocean, a seahorse couple is dancing.

The male swims around and around the female.

Another seahorse pair curls their tails together as they dance.

Soon, the male seahorses will do something that no other animal dads can do!

Seahorses are a type of small fish.
They live in the ocean, close to seashores.

A leafy seadragon seahorse

Head

Tail

Seahorses live among seaweed and ocean plants, and on rock-like **corals**.

Scientists have discovered 46 different types of seahorses.

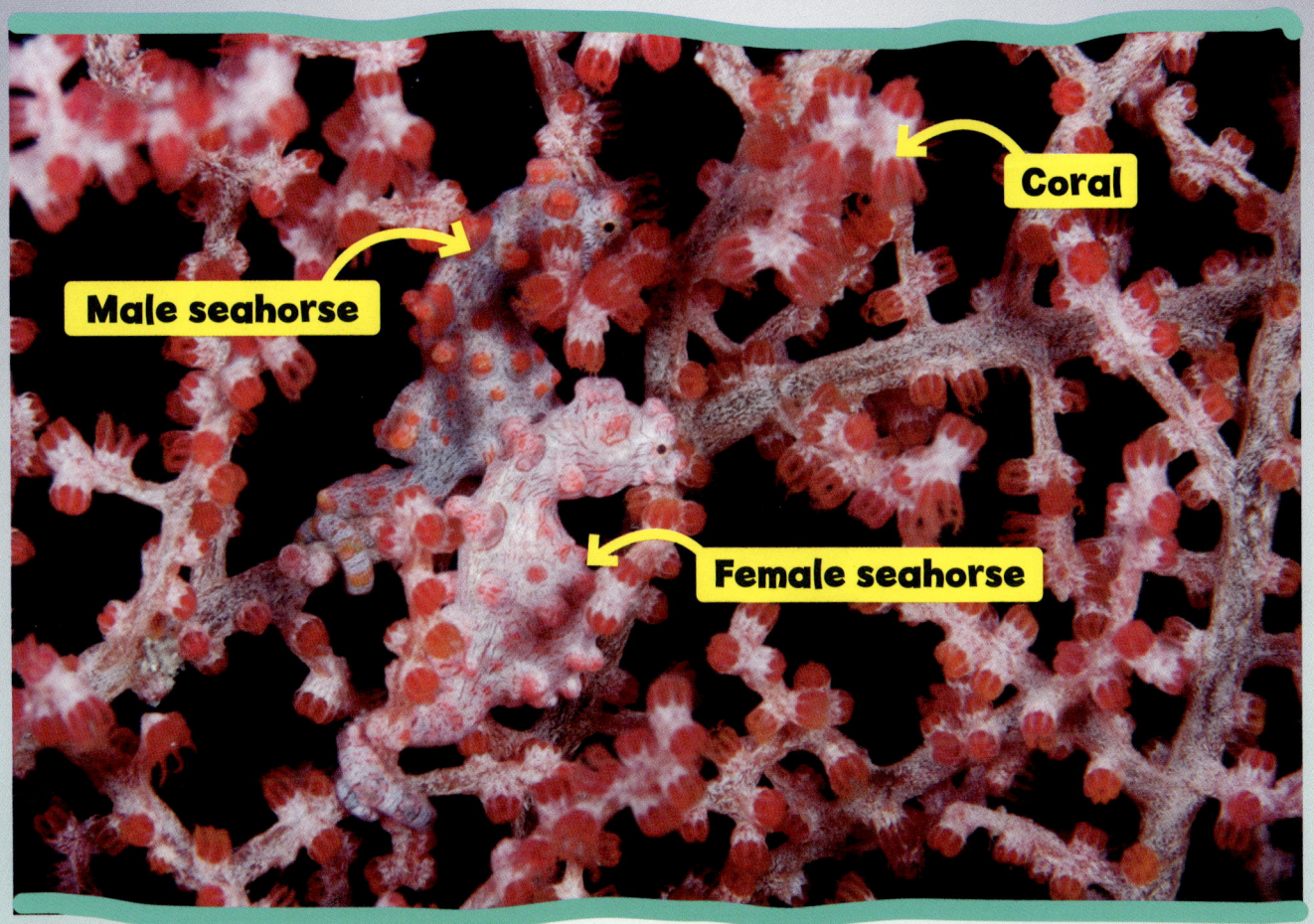

Some are very difficult to spot!

A seahorse holds onto plants, seaweed, and coral with its long bendy tail.

A seahorse has very good eyesight.

One eye can look backward while the other eye looks forward.

This helps it spot food.

Eye

Long snout

Seahorses suck up food with their long snouts. They eat tiny shrimp and worms.

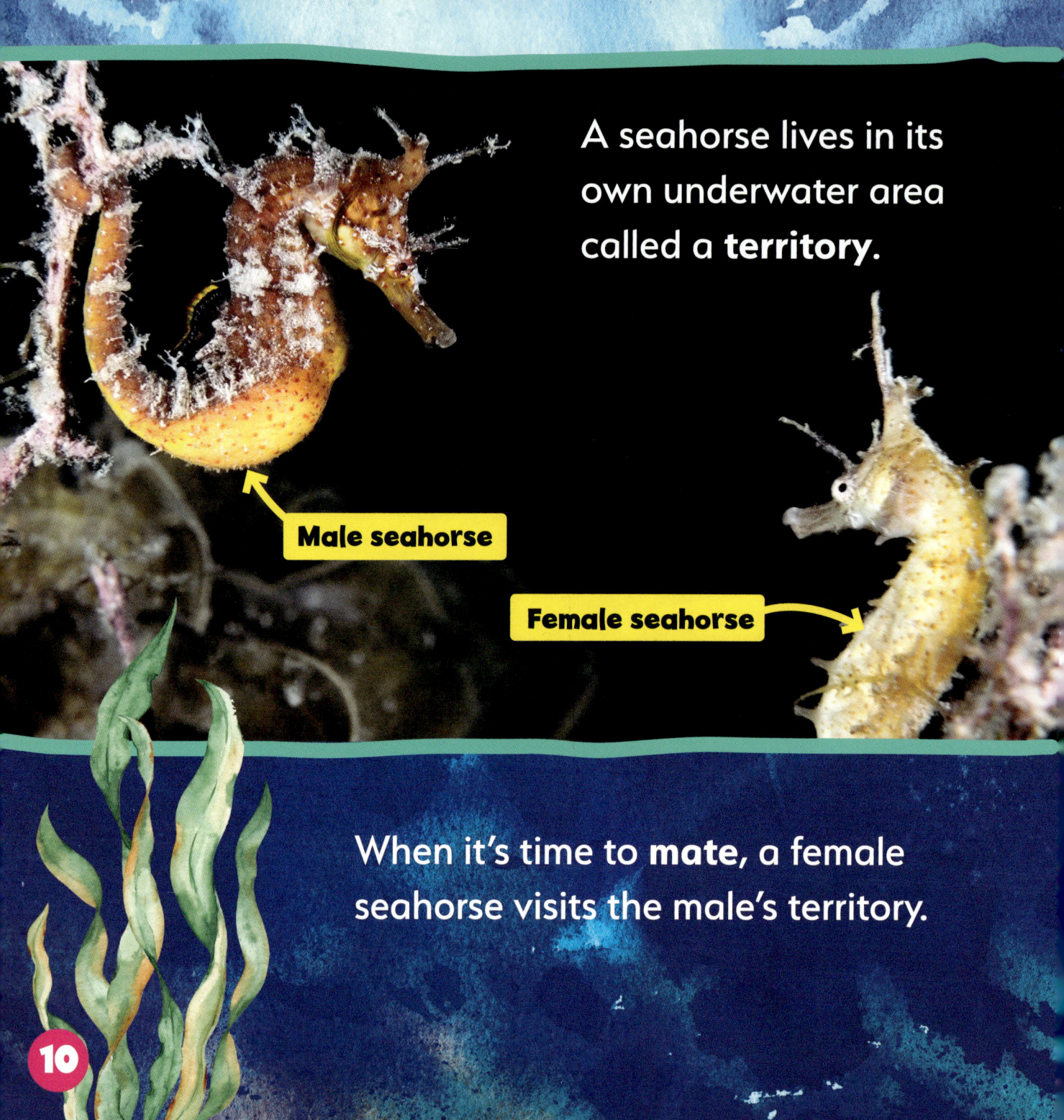

A seahorse lives in its own underwater area called a **territory**.

Male seahorse

Female seahorse

When it's time to **mate**, a female seahorse visits the male's territory.

She visits every morning to dance with her partner.

The dance is called a **courtship** dance.

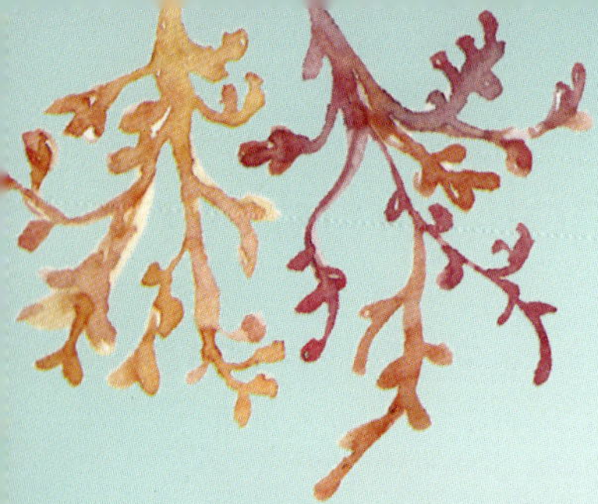

One morning, the seahorse pair mates.

The female passes her eggs into a **pouch** on the male's body.

The eggs mix with **sperm** in the male seahorse's pouch.

Now the eggs are ready to grow into baby seahorses.

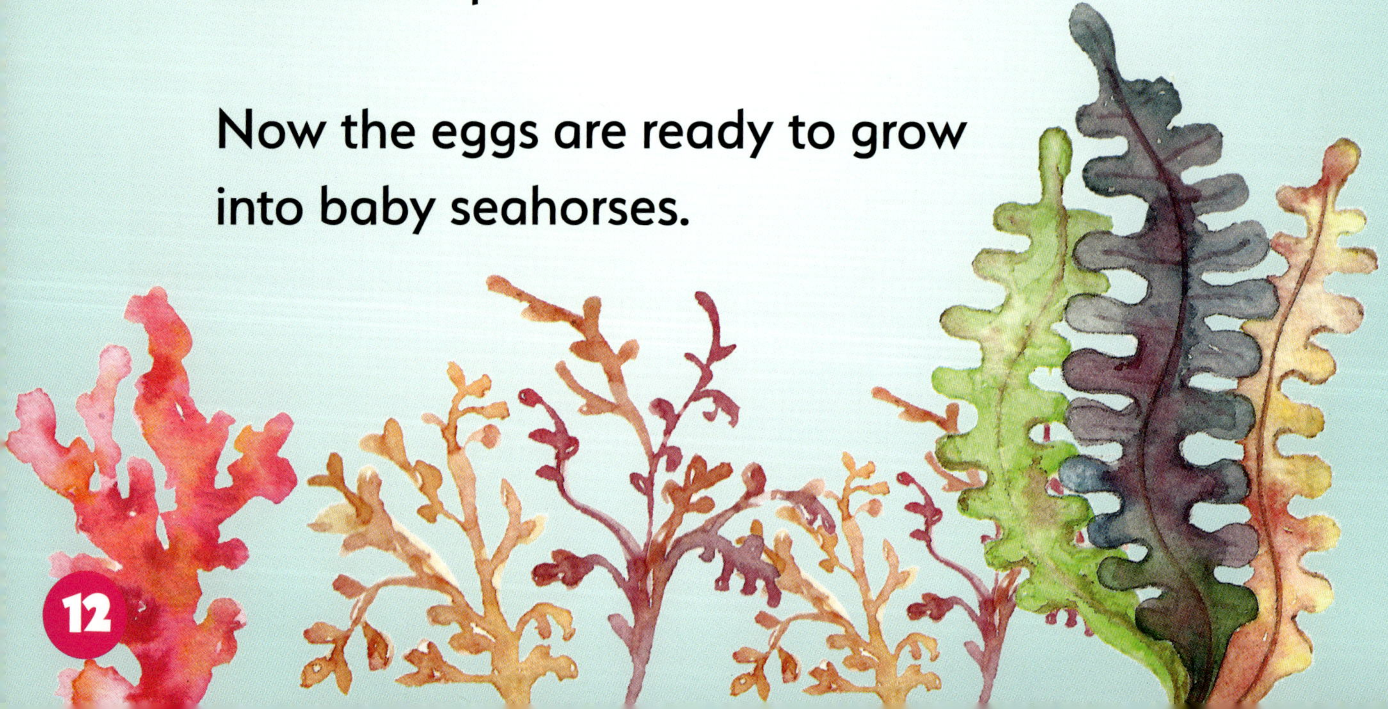

The father seahorse is now pregnant!

Inside the pouch, his tiny babies grow.

His body helps the babies breathe and be strong.

Each day, the mom seahorse visits to dance with the pregnant dad.

Pregnant father

A father seahorse may be pregnant for about six weeks.

One day, the father seahorse gives birth.

Father seahorse

Push! Push! Push!

Baby

He pushes tiny baby seahorses from his pouch.

A baby seahorse is just a little longer than a grain of rice.

A baby seahorse

Some types of father seahorses give birth to 1,500 babies!

A baby seahorse is called a fry.

It floats in the ocean.

Baby seahorses

A seahorse fry eats mini ocean animals.

After a few weeks, the little seahorses live in seaweed and ocean plants.

Floating food

Ocean plants

The father and mother seahorse do not take care of their babies. Why?

Baby seahorses can take care of themselves.

And the father seahorse has something important to do.

He is ready to have more babies.

Soon this amazing animal dad will mate and be pregnant again!

Glossary

corals
Tiny ocean animals that live and grow together. Their hard shells create rock-like places where other animals can live.

courtship
The things animals do to attract or please a partner before mating.

mate
To come together to produce young, or babies.

pouch
A pocket-like part of an animal's body where babies grow or are carried.

sperm
A substance made by male animals inside their bodies that helps make babies.

Pouch

territory
A place where an animal lives and finds its food.

Index

B
baby seahorses 12, 14, 16–17, 18–19, 20–21

D
dancing 4–5, 11, 14

E
eggs 12
eyes 9

F
father seahorses 4–5, 7, 10–11, 12–13, 14–15, 16–17, 19, 20–21
food 9, 18

M
mating 10, 12–13
mother seahorses 4–5, 7, 10, 12–13, 14–15, 19, 21

P
pouches 12–13, 14, 16

T
tails 5, 6, 8
territories 10